Where's Ash?

A Search and Find Adventure

HOW TO USE
THIS BOOK:

Ash Ketchum is on an
adventure to find Pokémon
across the regions.
Spot Ash in every scene
and search for Pokémon
everywhere he goes.

ORCHARD BOOKS
Carmelite House, 50 Victoria Embankment, London EC4Y 0DZ
First published in 2021 by The Watts Publishing Group
ISBN 978 1 40836 389 8

A CIP catalogue record for this book is available from the British Library.

Printed in China 10 9 8 7 6 5 4 3

Orchard Books is an imprint of Hachette Children's Group
and published by Watts Publishing Group Limited,
an Hachette UK Company
www.hachette.co.uk
www.hachettechildrens.co.uk

This search and find book belongs to:

....

ORCHARD

THE SEARCH BEGINS

It's a beautiful day in Kanto. Ash is looking forward to meeting Squirtle, Bulbasaur and Charmander, who are going to show him around. Adventure awaits!

CAN YOU FIND?

| BELLSPROUT x2 | PONYTA | DODUO | METAPOD | ASH |

SUNSET SEARCH

Our hero, Ash, stops in a quiet spot to admire the sunset.
Exploring is exciting! Where to next?

CAN YOU FIND?

MACHOKE · VENOMOTH x3 · HITMONCHAN · EEVEE · SNORLAX · ASH

7

FOREST FINDER

Ash is searching the forest in Johto. Pokémon can be tricky to spot amongst the trees, can you help Ash on his mission?

CAN YOU FIND?

SLAKOTH   LOPUNNY   TOGETIC   BEEDRILL   BELLOSSOM   ASH

SAIL AND SPOT

Ash and Pikachu are sailing across a lake to the city.
Help them spot lots of Water-type Pokémon along the way.

CAN YOU FIND?

 CLAMPERL   **SWAMPERT**   **KINGDRA**   **FLOATZEL**   **MASQUERAIN**   **ASH**

11

HANGING OUT IN HOENN

Next, Ash explores the region of Hoenn. With Pikachu by his side, Ash travels through the forest, spots ancient ruins and heads towards the ocean.

CAN YOU FIND?

| LOTAD x2 | ROSELIA x2 | GROVYLE x2 | LILEEP | CACTURNE | ASH |

TIME TO REST

Our friends make a stopover at a reef.
See how many Water-type Pokémon you can spot as they rest.

CAN YOU FIND?

CLAMPERL | SWABLU | SPHEAL x2 | KYOGRE | LOTAD | ASH

SEARCHING SINNOH

It's a beautiful day in the mountains of Sinnoh. Ash and Pikachu are meeting many new Pokémon. Help them to search the area.

CAN YOU FIND?

BUIZEL PIPLUP TURTWIG CROAGUNK SUDOWOODO ASH

17

FIND THE FLYERS

Have you ever seen so many Flying-type Pokémon?
This is the perfect opportunity for Ash to discover what's on his list.

CAN YOU FIND?

ROTOM   PELIPPER ×4   TOGEKISS   SKORUPI   YANMEGA ×2   ASH

NIGHT-TIME MISSION

By the time they arrive in Unova, night has fallen.
It's the perfect time to spot lots of Dark-type Pokemon.

CAN YOU FIND?

DWEBBLE x5 · KLINK · YAMASK x2 · MUSHARNA · ASH

21

PREPARE TO BATTLE

Ash is visiting a training room in Unova to practise before he signs up for a Gym battle. It looks like he has some serious competition!

CAN YOU FIND?

 TRANQUILL

 PANSAGE

 PANSEAR

 PANPOUR

 AUDINO

 ASH

FLOWERY FINDINGS

This area of the Kalos region is full of flowers.
Ash thinks this is the most beautiful region so far.

CAN YOU FIND?

EEVEE • SYLVEON • PANGORO • PICHU • GOGOAT • LITLEO • ASH

SEARCH BY STARLIGHT

It's Umbreon, the Dark-type Pokémon! Ash can't believe his luck.
Find the Pokémon on his list on this beautiful starry night.

CAN YOU FIND?

UMBREON   SABLEYE ×3   ZOROARK ×2   GOOMY   HONEDGE   ASH

OUT IN ALOLA

Ash's adventures have led him to the Alola region and the guardian
of the Mele-Mele island appears. What could this mean?

CAN YOU FIND?

BOUNSWEET · ALOLAN GRIMER · ALOLAN EXEGGUTOR · VIKAVOLT · CATERPIE · ASH

ICY ADVENTURE

Next, Ash ventures to the Alolan island of Ula-Ula and climbs a tall mountain.
Look, Ice-type Pokémon!

CAN YOU FIND?

- TAPU BULU
- ALOLAN SANDSHREW
- ALOLAN VULPIX ×5
- DRIFLOON
- ASH

WELCOME TO GALAR

Ash and Pikachu arrive in Galar and there are so many new friends to spot.
How many new Pokémon can you find?

CAN YOU FIND?

ETERNATUS GOSSIFLEUR NICKIT GREEDENT FLAPPLE ASH

ANSWERS

POKÉMON

ASH

PAGES 4 - 5

THE SEARCH BEGINS

PAGES 6 - 7

SUNSET SEARCH

FOREST FINDER

PAGES 8 - 9

SAIL AND SPOT

HANGING OUT IN HOENN

TIME TO REST

SEARCHING SINNOH

FIND THE FLYERS

PAGES 18 - 19

PAGES 20 - 21

NIGHT-TIME MISSION

PREPARE TO BATTLE

PAGES 22 - 23

PAGES 24 - 25

FLOWERY FINDINGS

SEARCH BY STARLIGHT

PAGES 26 - 27

PAGES 28 - 29

OUT IN ALOLA

ICY ADVENTURE

PAGES 30 - 31

PAGES 32 - 33

WELCOME TO GALAR

CHECK OUT THESE OTHER POKÉMON SEARCH AND FIND BOOKS